Windows

MOVIE MAKER & YOU

Turn Your Photos into a DVD Slideshow –
It's *Easier* Than You Think!

By Jean Tennant

A Just-the-Basics guide to creating
fun movies to share with friends and family.

Published by: Shapato Publishing
PO Box 476
Everly, IA 51338

ISBN: 978-0-9821058-5-6
Library of Congress Control Number: 2009909005
Copyright © 2009 Shapato Publishing

All rights reserved. No part of this book may be reproduced or transmitted in any form or by any means, electronic or mechanical, including photocopying, recording, or by an information storage and retrieval system, without permission in writing from the publisher.

First Printing September 2009

Microsoft product screen shots reprinted with permission from Microsoft Corporation.

Music used in slideshow presentation:
"See You There" by Chad Elliott
www.ChadElliott.net
Used with permission.

INTRODUCTION

Several years ago I started a small business called Remember When…Keepsake Videos. I kept busy (and had fun) creating DVD slideshows for graduations, weddings, anniversaries— just about any occasion you can imagine. It was challenging work but always enjoyable, and put me in touch with people who have remained my friends to this day.

During that time I learned to use Windows Movie Maker, mostly by stumbling around in the dark and figuring it out myself. But as it's a very user-friendly program, even a novice (at the time) as myself was able to use it to full advantage. As my skills improved I decided I needed something fancier (i.e. expensive) than the free Movie Maker program. I bought one, then another, and eventually ended up going back to the original program, wiser for the experience and more appreciative than ever of Windows Movie Maker.

After a few years of this I found that my writing, which I've been doing professionally for more than thirty years, and my publishing business were taking up so much of my time that I no longer had time to create movies for other people. But I continue to do it for myself and my family because, once learned, this is a skill simply too much fun to give up.

This guide is intended to give you the basic knowledge to get started with Windows Movie Maker. There are more bells and whistles to the program than I list here, but once you gain some confidence and create a couple of movies of your own, I have no doubt you'll explore and experiment, as I did.

I hope you'll enjoy creating your own movies to share with your friends and family as much as I have.

Jean Tennant

TABLE OF CONTENTS

Introduction	3
Open Windows Movie Maker	8
Import Images	10
Add Images to Storyboard	12
Title and End Credits	14
Title Animation	16
Transitions	20
Video Effects	28
Add Video	30
Music	34
Narration	38
End Credits	40
Save Your Movie File	42
Burn Your Movie to a DVD	46
Ta-da!	48

Windows

MOVIE MAKER & YOU

Turn Your Photos into a DVD Slideshow –
It's *Easier* Than You Think!

By Jean Tennant

LET'S GET STARTED!

OPEN WINDOWS MOVIE MAKER

First find Windows Movie Maker, most commonly located in your Programs file. Go to START in the lower left corner of your computer, open ALL PROGRAMS.

Windows Movie Maker is indicated by the icon: or:

This would be a good time to save Movie Maker to your desktop for easy access, since you no doubt will be using it often from now on.

Once Movie Maker is open, if you don't see MOVIE TASKS in the area to the left of your screen, go to VIEW at the top of the page and within the drop-down box click on TASK PANE. While you're there, it's a good idea now to also open TOOLBAR and STATUS BAR.

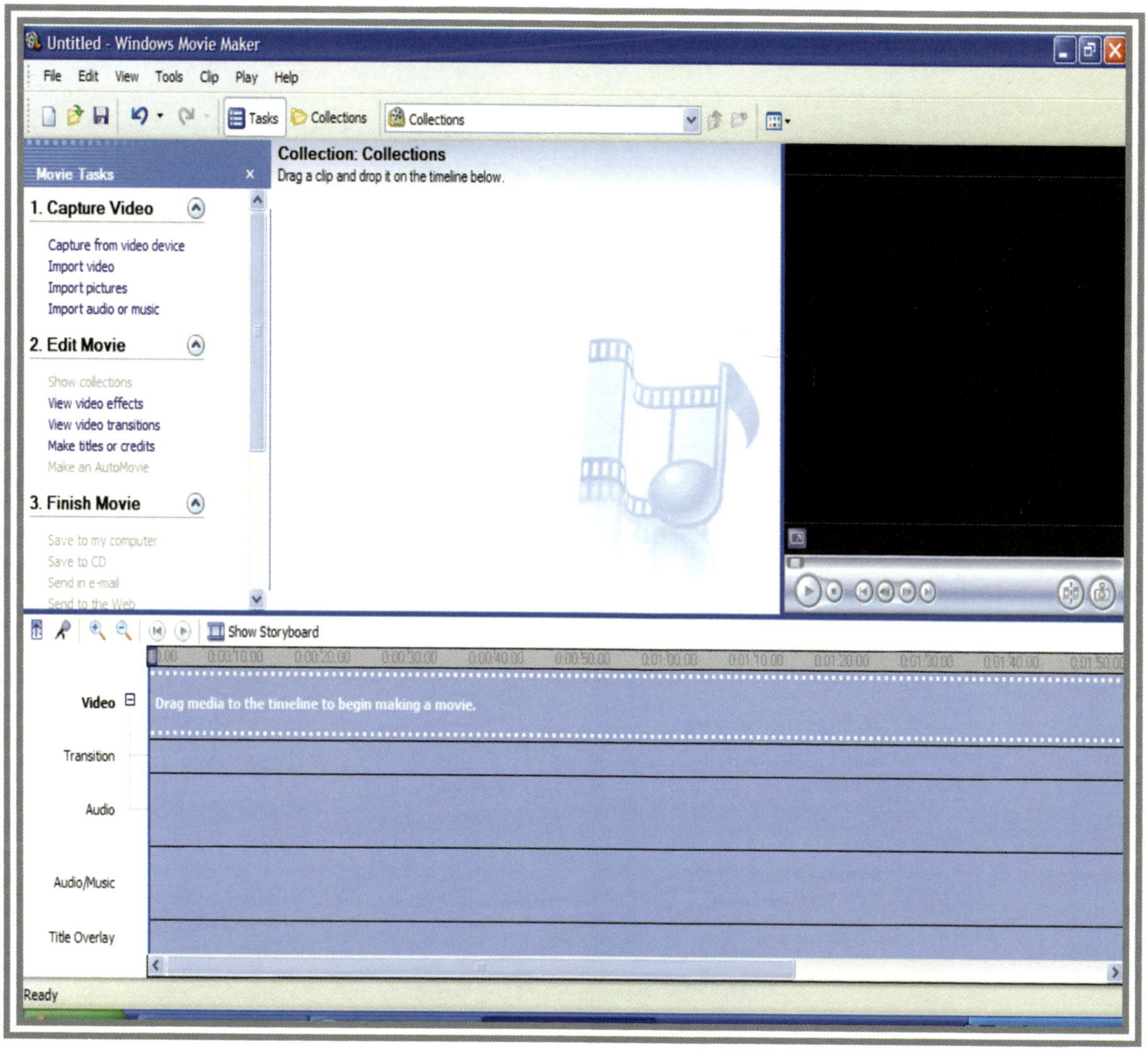
Untitled - Windows Movie Maker
File Edit View Tools Clip Play Help
Tasks
Collections
Collections
Movie Tasks
Collection: Collections
Drag a clip and drop it on the timeline below.
1. Capture Video
Capture from video device
Import video
Import pictures
Import audio or music
2. Edit Movie
Show collections
View video effects
View video transitions
Make titles or credits
Make an AutoMovie
3. Finish Movie
Save to my computer
Save to CD
Send in e-mail
Send to the Web
Show Storyboard
Video
Drag media to the timeline to begin making a movie.
Transition
Audio
Audio/Music
Title Overlay
Ready

IMPORT IMAGES

You're now ready to create a new Movie Maker slideshow presentation.

Add digital photos to your slideshow by clicking on IMPORT PICTURES in MOVIE TASKS.

When the IMPORT FILE box opens, choose which photos from your files you wish to add to your slideshow. For better viewing, make sure the VIEW MENU icon on the far right is on THUMBNAILS. This allows you to see the images you want to import, rather than relying on the image name alone.

To import multiple images, simply click on one image, then hold the CTRL key down on your computer keyboard as you click on more. When you've chosen all the images you want, click on IMPORT. All of the images you selected will be imported to your COLLECTIONS.

> Old photographs (as in pre-digital) can be added to your slideshow as well. Simply scan them and save them on your computer, then import the same as above.

At this time it's a good idea to name your project. Click on FILE in the upper left corner, and from the dropdown box select SAVE PROJECT AS. Here you'll name your project, and you'll also choose the folder in which you wish to save it. The default setting is in the MY VIDEOS folder, but you can save it wherever you wish.

> There are always two people in every picture: the photographer and the viewer.
> ~ Ansel Adams

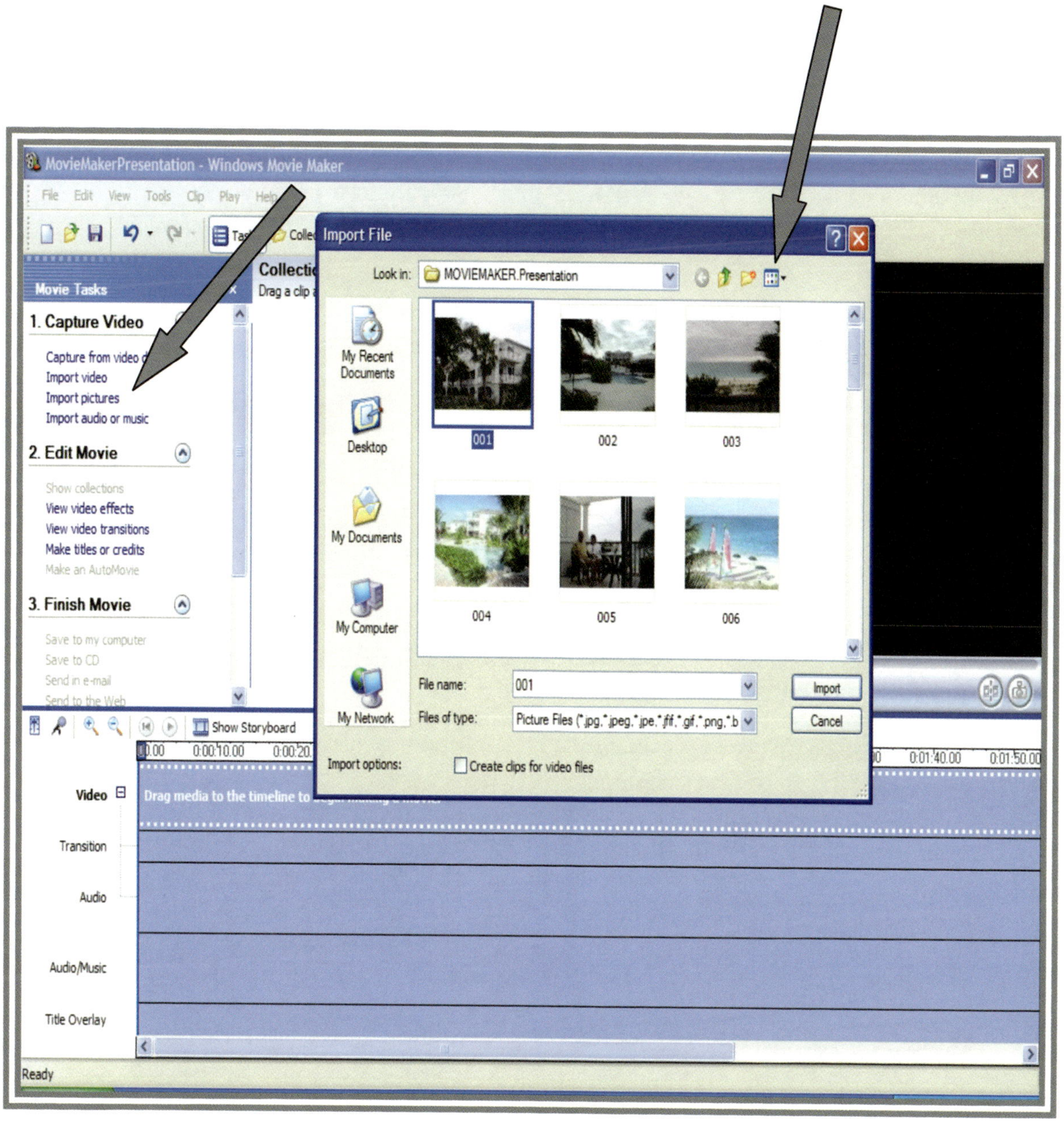
MovieMakerPresentation - Windows Movie Maker
File Edit View Tools Clip Play Help
Movie Tasks
1. Capture Video
Capture from video
Import video
Import pictures
Import audio or music
2. Edit Movie
Show collections
View video effects
View video transitions
Make titles or credits
Make an AutoMovie
3. Finish Movie
Save to my computer
Save to CD
Send in e-mail
Send to the Web
Import File
Look in: MOVIEMAKER.Presentation
My Recent Documents
Desktop
My Documents
My Computer
My Network
001
002
003
004
005
006
File name: 001
Files of type: Picture Files (*.jpg,*.jpeg,*.jpe,*.jfif,*.gif,*.png,*.b
Import
Cancel
Import options:
Create clips for video files
Show Storyboard
Video
Transition
Audio
Audio/Music
Title Overlay
Ready

ADD IMAGES TO STORYBOARD

Highlight all of your photos and drag them as one down to the VIDEO portion of your storyboard. Movie Maker will insert all of your photos for you, in order.

> To drag all of your imported images to the Storyboard, go up to EDIT, and SELECT ALL. This will highlight all of the images in your Collections.

Above your video strip you'll see STORYBOARD. If you click on this it will change your setting to TIMELINE. I prefer to keep it on STORYBOARD all the time.

To the left of that you'll see two little magnifying glasses with + and – symbols. Click on these to increase or decrease the size of your images in the STORYBOARD. This comes in handy. When you're adding Transitions it's easier to see what you're doing if you enlarge the images a bit. This does not, however, change the length of time each image lasts in the slideshow.

When you place your cursor over an image you'll see the image name, as well as the duration that image will be displayed. The default setting in this case is 6 seconds. You can change the default setting by going to TOOLS at the top of your page, then OPTIONS. In the Options box click on the ADVANCED tab, where you'll see PICTURE DURATION, and the number of seconds.

However, it's just as easy to change the duration of your image in your STORYBOARD by placing your cursor on the right edge of the image and dragging it to the length you want.

13

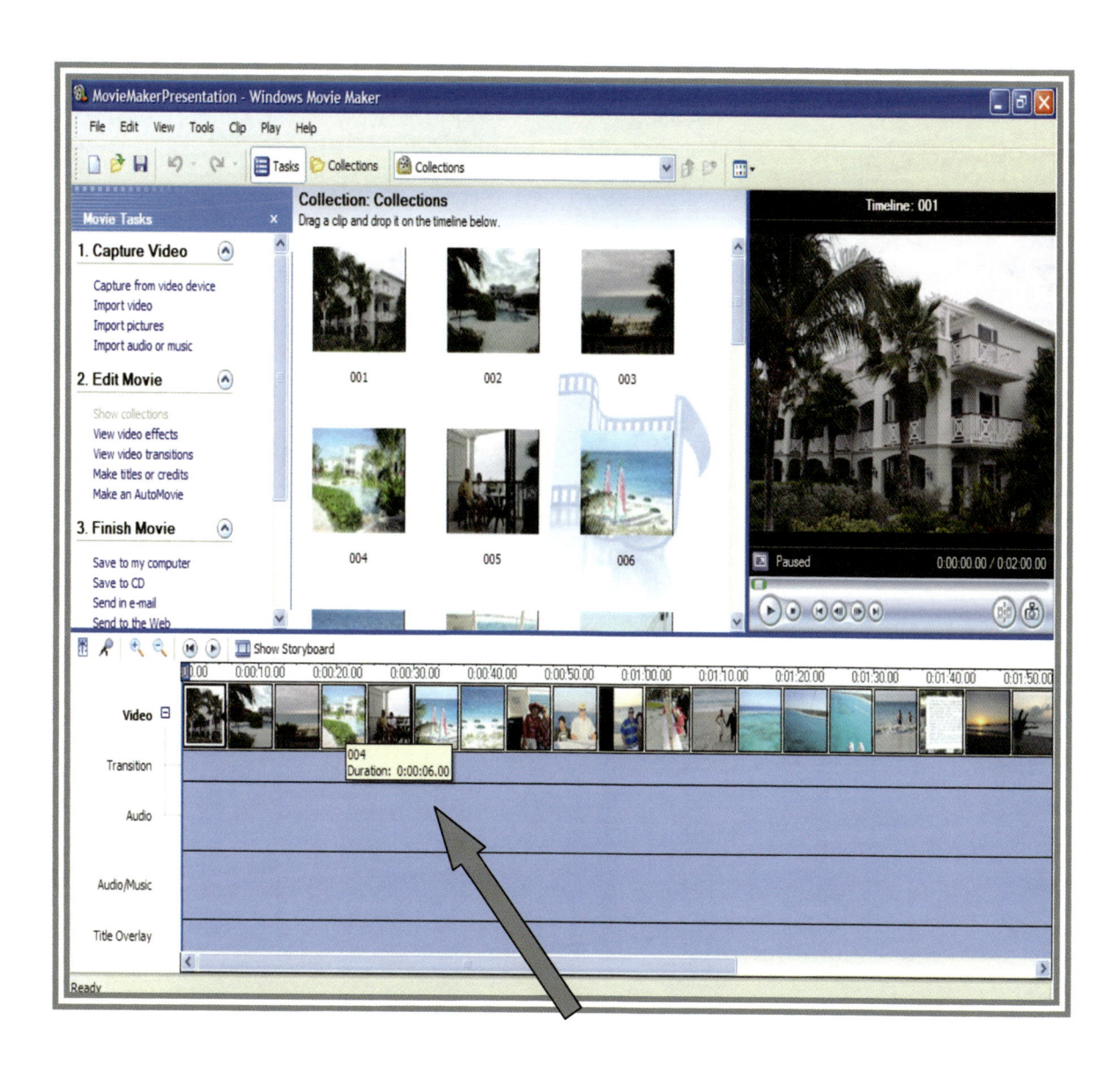

TITLE AND END CREDITS

In your Movie Tasks section click on MAKE TITLES OR CREDITS. For our purposes here we'll use TITLE AT THE BEGINNING of the movie.

You can, of course, add title pages anywhere in your slideshow you wish.

> **A good snapshot stops a moment from running away.**
> *~Eudora Welty*

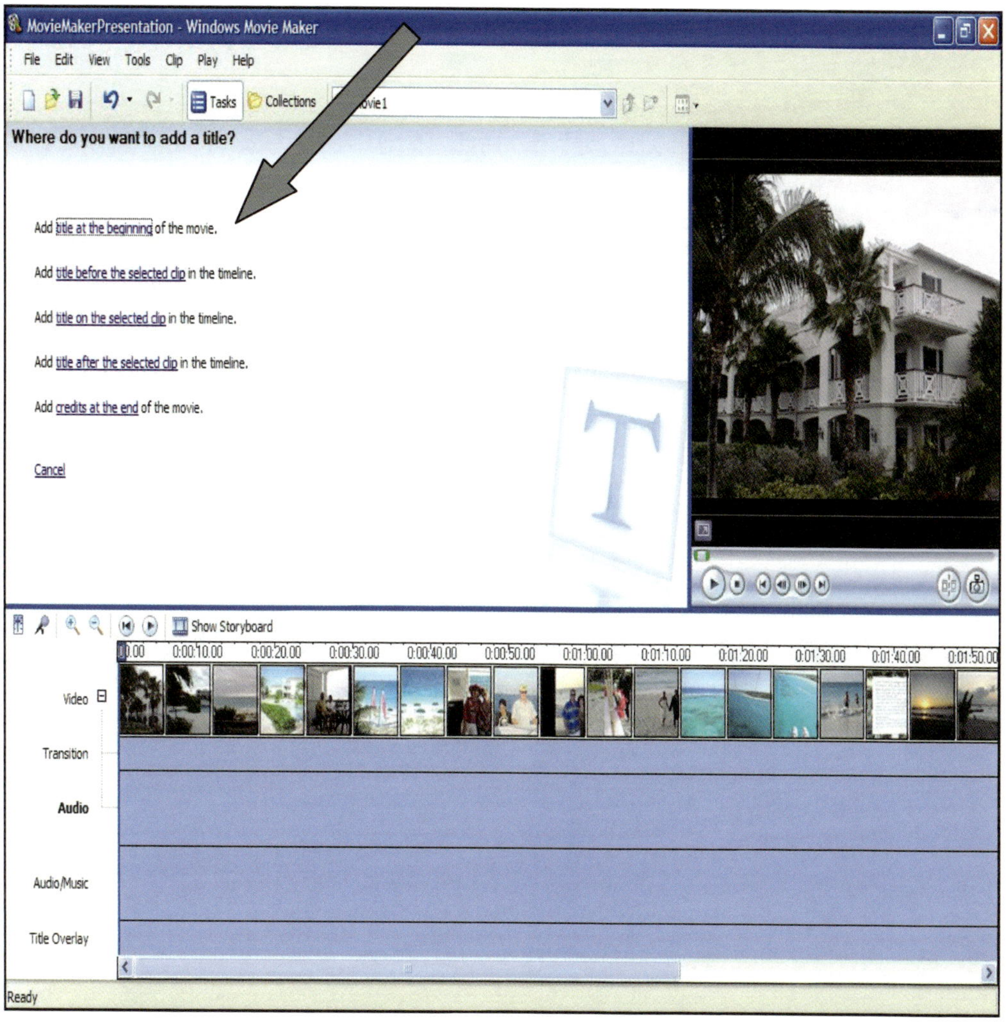
MovieMakerPresentation - Windows Movie Maker
File Edit View Tools Clip Play Help
Tasks
Collections
Where do you want to add a title?
Add title at the beginning of the movie.
Add title before the selected clip in the timeline.
Add title on the selected clip in the timeline.
Add title after the selected clip in the timeline.
Add credits at the end of the movie.
Cancel
Show Storyboard
Video
Transition
Audio
Audio/Music
Title Overlay
Ready

TITLE ANIMATION

A box called ENTER TEXT FOR TITLE will appear. Add the text you want to appear on the first page of your slideshow.

Below that box you'll see CHANGE THE TITLE ANIMATION. Click on that, and you'll be presented with a bunch of options for your Title Animation. Play with them for a bit; experiment until you find one you like. You can change it at any time during the creation of your slideshow.

There are more than forty (both one and two-lines) Titles and Credits to choose from. My favorite happens to be MOVING TITLE, LAYERED. It has a fun, flowing look that works well as the lead-in to most projects.

Next go to CHANGE THE TEXT FONT AND COLOR. Here you'll choose the Font you wish to use for your slideshow, as well as the color and size. I like *Monotype Corsiva*, but there are, incredibly, more than 250 fonts to choose from. I've used *Chiller* when creating a Halloween slideshow, and *Andy* for a more playful look.

Select your background color. You can also adjust the Transparency, and Center your text or Right or Left justify.

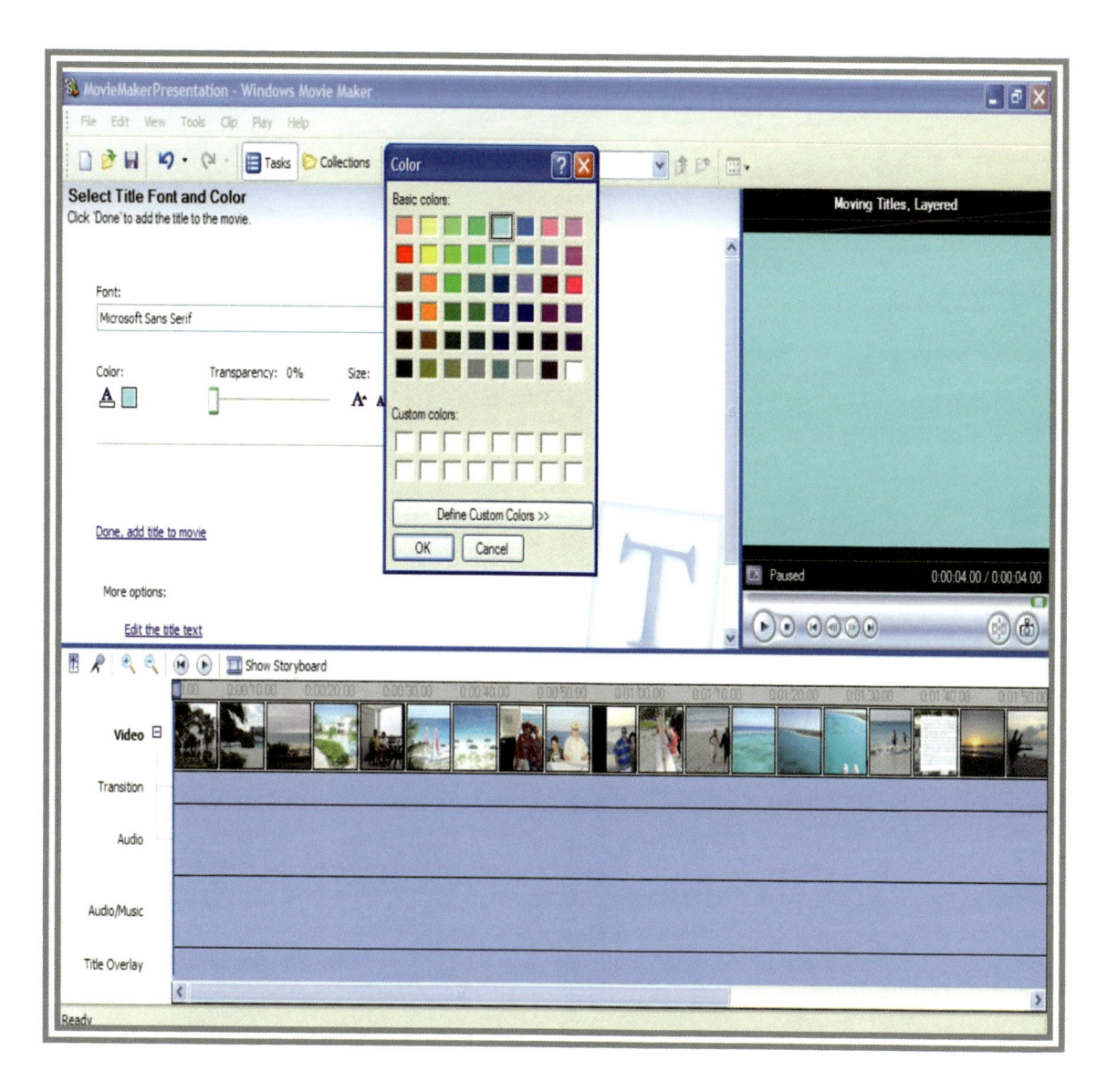

You can tweak the basic colors offered by going to Define Custom Colors.

When you're finished, click on DONE, ADD TITLE TO MOVIE.

As I mentioned, you can change any of these details at any time. You're not locked into anything until the end.

Now that you've added the Title Page to your slideshow, there's another thing to know—when your slideshow starts, it begins rather abruptly with the Title Page.

To begin your slideshow a bit more gracefully, place your cursor directly on the Title Page and *Right Click* on it. An EDIT TITLE box will open. Choose FADE IN. A Star will appear on the Title Page. This indicates a transition, and in this case the FADE IN transition. This is a nice way to begin your slideshow.

> The creative act lasts but a brief moment, a lightning instant of give-and-take, just long enough for you to level the camera and to trap the fleeting prey in your little box.
> ~Henri Cartier Bresson

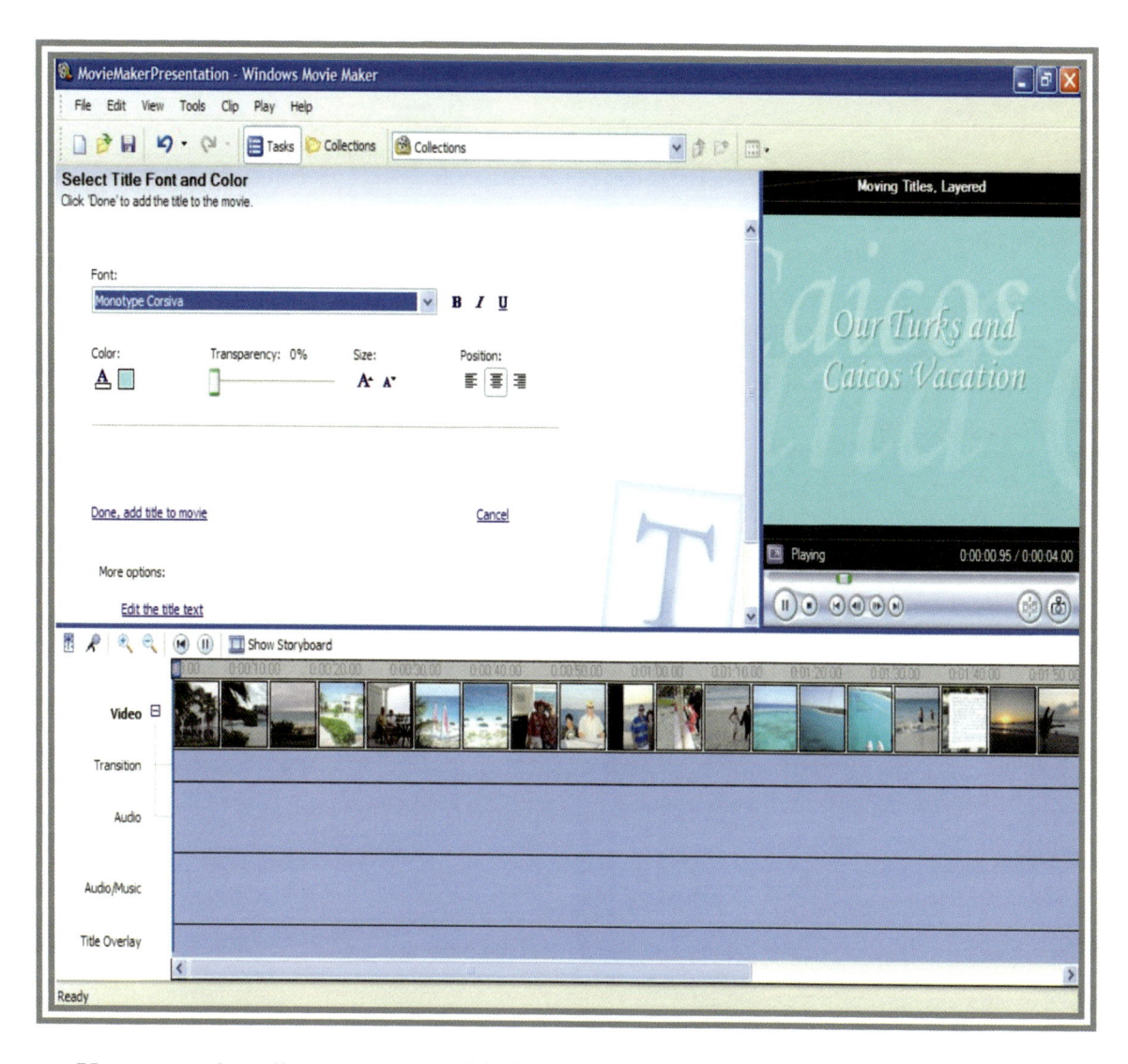

You can make adjustments your title by selecting SIZE to make the font larger or smaller; and POSITION to center, right or left on the page.

TRANSITIONS

Transitions are fun! But a word of caution: don't overdo it. A nice overlap/fade is the best choice between most of your images, with only a few fancy transitions thrown in to jazz things up.

> A slideshow with a fancy transition between every image becomes a distraction. Your viewers will be looking at the transitions and wondering what's coming next. You want them looking at your *pictures*, and thinking how wonderful they are!

Place your cursor squarely on an image and drag that image to the *Left*. This will create a nice overlap between it and the previous image. Make the duration as long as you wish, keeping in mind the longer the duration the slower the fade. Also, don't overlap so much that your image doesn't get enough screen time of its own.

The PLAYBACK INDICATOR is the vertical blue line on your slideshow. Whichever image it rests on is the one that appears in the screen to the right of your work area.

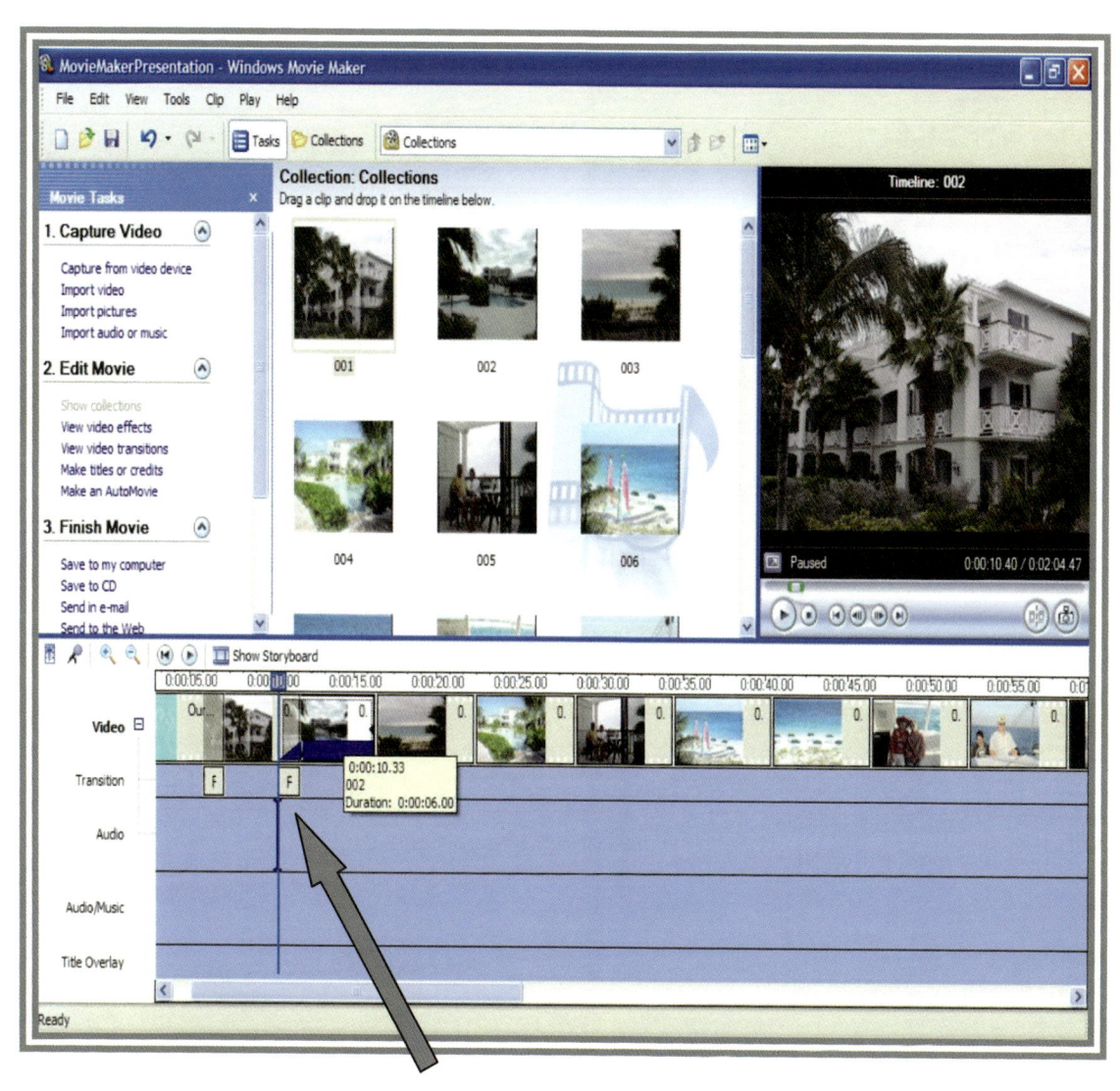

A one- to two-second transition overlap is your best choice.

This is also a good time to change the viewing time of your individual images, if you wish.

To increase the length of time your image appears in your slideshow, place your cursor on the Right edge of the image and drag it to the *Right*.

To decrease the length of time your image appears, place your cursor on the Right edge of the image and drag it to the *Left*.

As mentioned earlier, the default setting for the length of time your image appears is usually set at 6 seconds, but you can change that to whatever you want. Remember, go to TOOLS, and in the drop-down choose OPTIONS. Select the ADVANCED tab, and there you will see the Picture Duration setting.

Changing the default setting won't affect the images you've already added to your Storyboard, but it will change the duration of any images you add from this point on.

> Beauty can be seen in all things. Seeing and composing the beauty is what separates the snapshot from the photograph.
> ~ *Matt Hardy*

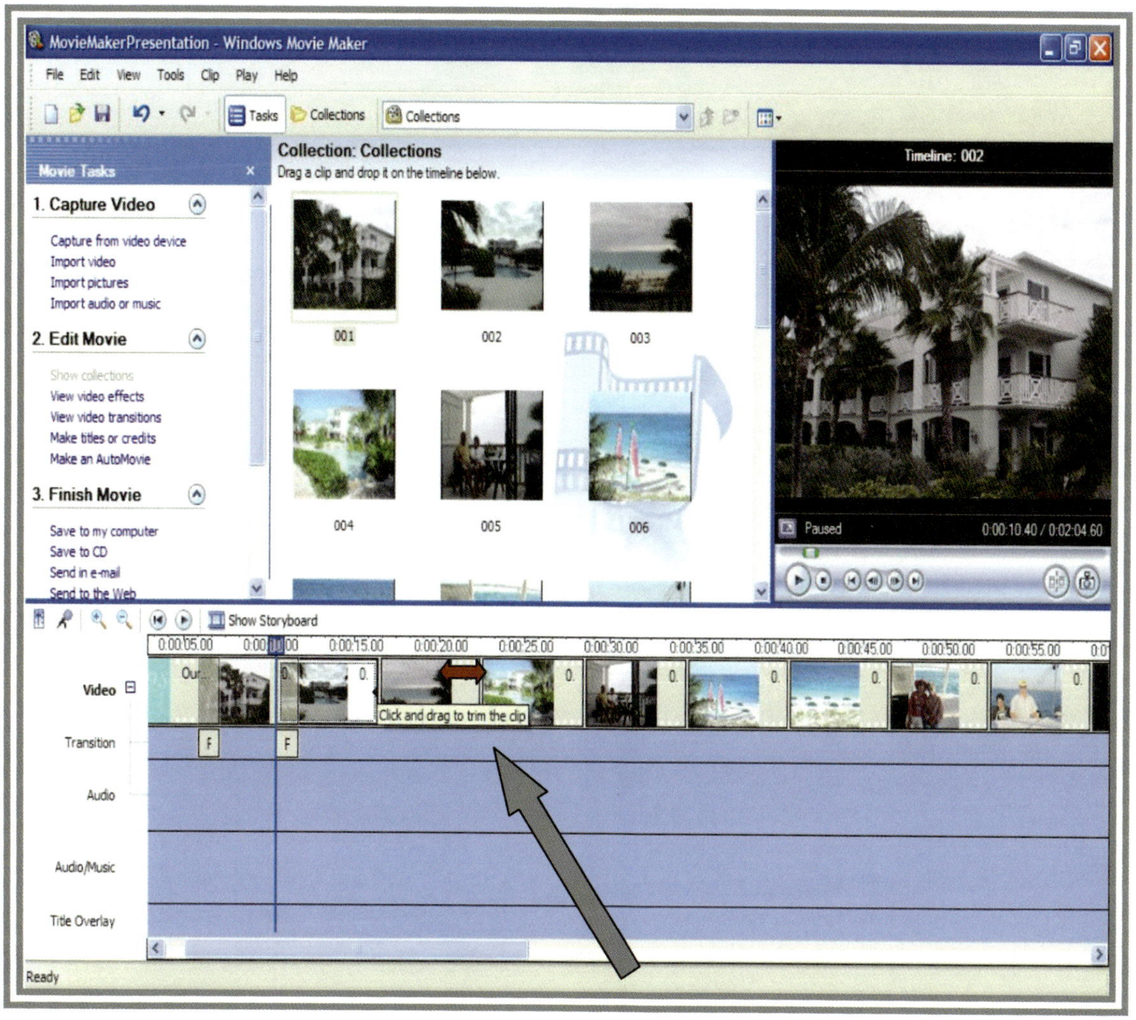

To choose your fancy transitions, click on VIEW VIDEO TRANSITIONS in Movie Tasks.

Look at all those great transitions! It's tempting to go crazy and use one between every image in your slideshow, but resist that temptation if you can. Too many fancy transitions draw attention away from your photographs, which is not what you want. It's best to stick with a simple Fade/Overlap between images, with fancy transitions being used only occasionally.

A good rule of thumb is to incorporate a transition before every sixth to tenth image, depending on the overall length of the slideshow.

> You don't have to use any transitions if you prefer not to, of course, but if you don't, you will want to at least have each image fade in and fade out. If your slideshow moves from one image to the next with no transition and no fade it will create an abrupt change that's visually jarring.

To choose one of the Transitions in Movie Maker, simply place your cursor on it and drag it down to where you want it.

There are a few Transitions that have, over the years, become my favorites:

> The Circle works well early in the slideshow, especially after the title page.
>
> The Page Curl, Up Right has a nice, elegant look that goes well with wedding and graduation slideshows, especially before a picture of a person in formalwear. Extend the length of the transition so the Page Curl moves slowly.
>
> And for a dramatic ending to your slideshow, you can't beat Shatter In. Use it right before the final photo image of your slideshow, extending it to about 3 seconds in length for full effect. Since it will eat up 3 seconds of your final image, don't forget to increase the length of that, as well.

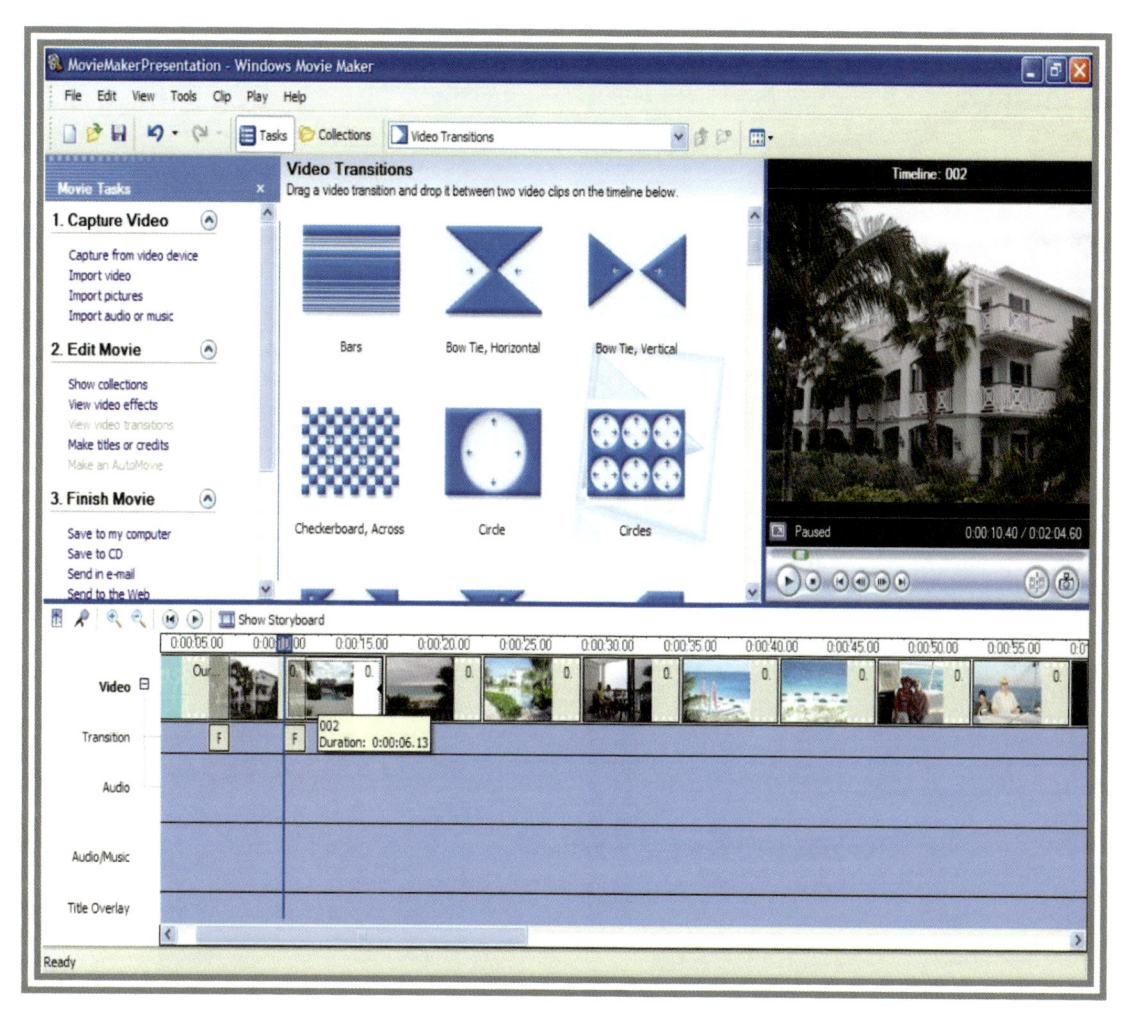

Experiment with different transitions. You'll soon settle on your favorites.

At this point you should be viewing your slideshow occasionally to see how it looks with the Title Page and Transitions.

To do this click on the PLAY button in the lower left corner of the viewer. This will begin your slideshow, and you'll start to get an idea of how the finished product will look.

> If you want to make an apple pie from scratch, you must first create the universe.
>   - *Carl Sagan*

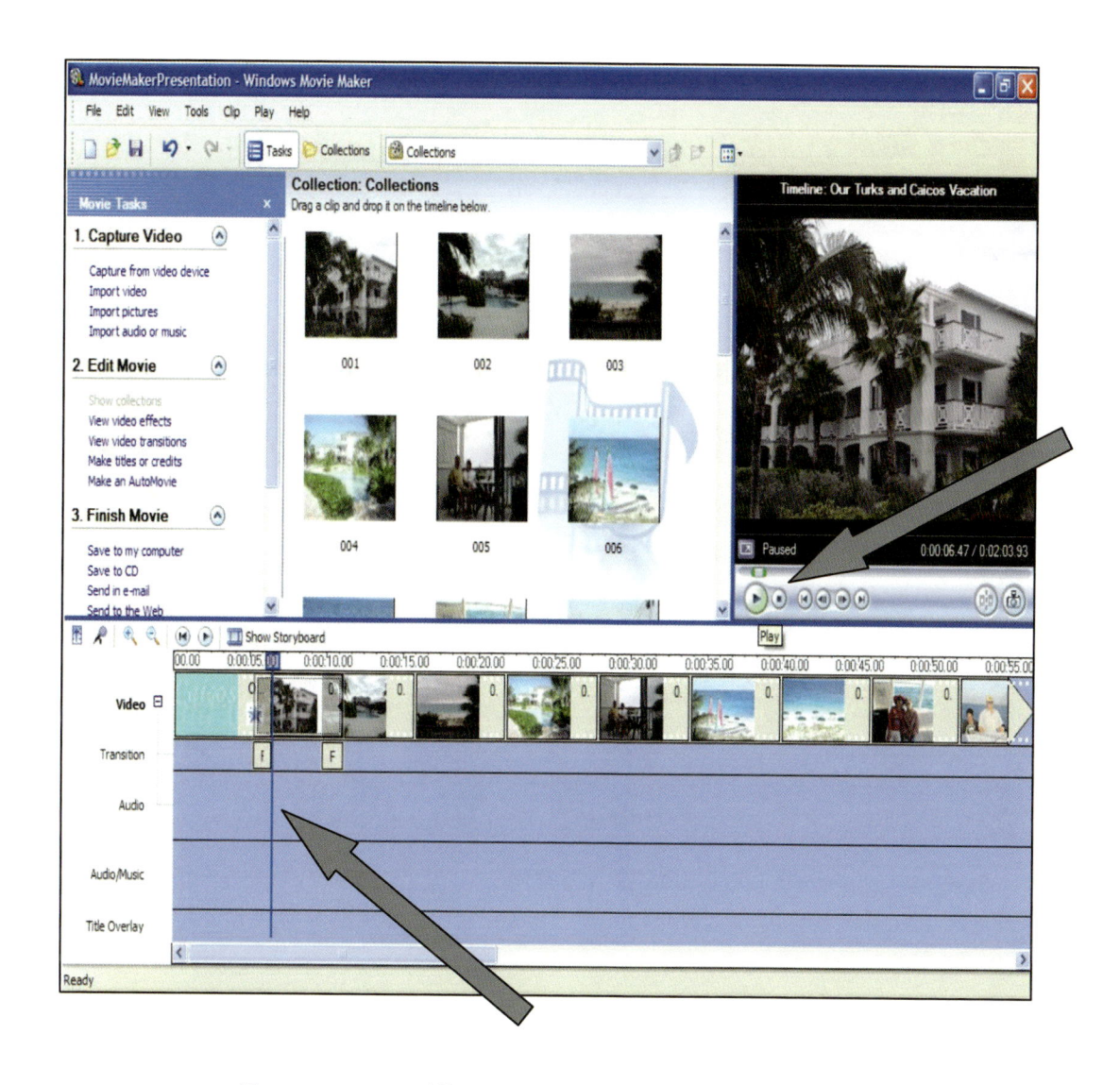

To get to a specific spot in your slideshow, move the PLAYBACK INDICATOR to where you want to go.

27

VIDEO EFFECTS

Like Transitions, VIDEO EFFECTS are a lot of fun, but should be used sparingly. To choose an effect, place your cursor on it and drag it down to the chosen image.

> After you've been in Video Transitions and Video Effects, to return to your images click on Show Collections in your MOVIE TASKS area.

To add a VIDEO EFFECT to an individual image, simply drag it down to that image as you did with Transitions. You might use Ease Out on an image to make it slowly move away from the screen, or Ease In for it to move slowly forward.

If you want to create an old-fashioned look for your movie, use Film Age, Old or Film Age, Older.

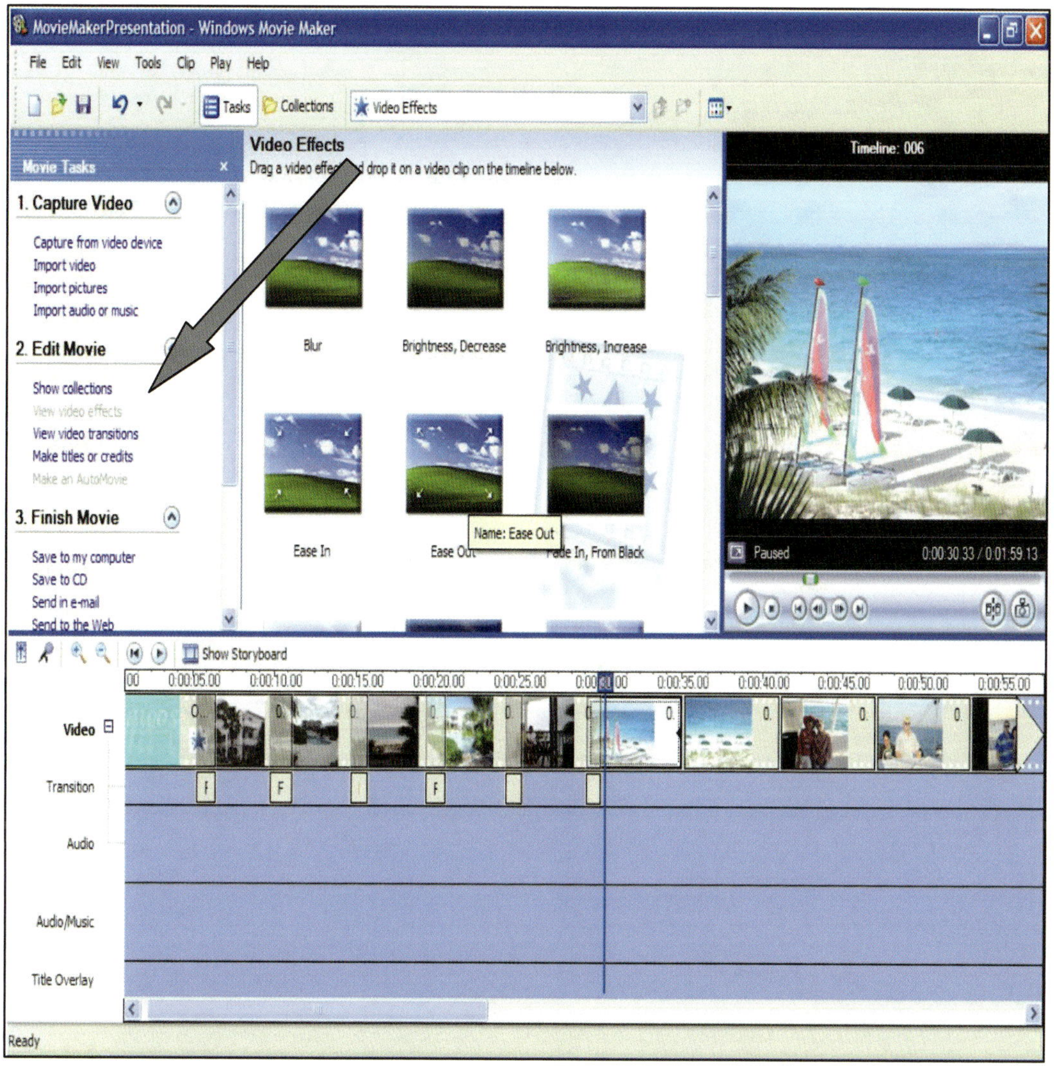

ADD VIDEO

There's no need to limit yourself to still photos in your slideshow. You can add video as well.

In your MOVIE TASKS area, click on IMPORT VIDEO. Find your video in the folder in which you have it stored, and Import.

> Life is the movie you see through your own eyes.
> ~ Denis Waitley

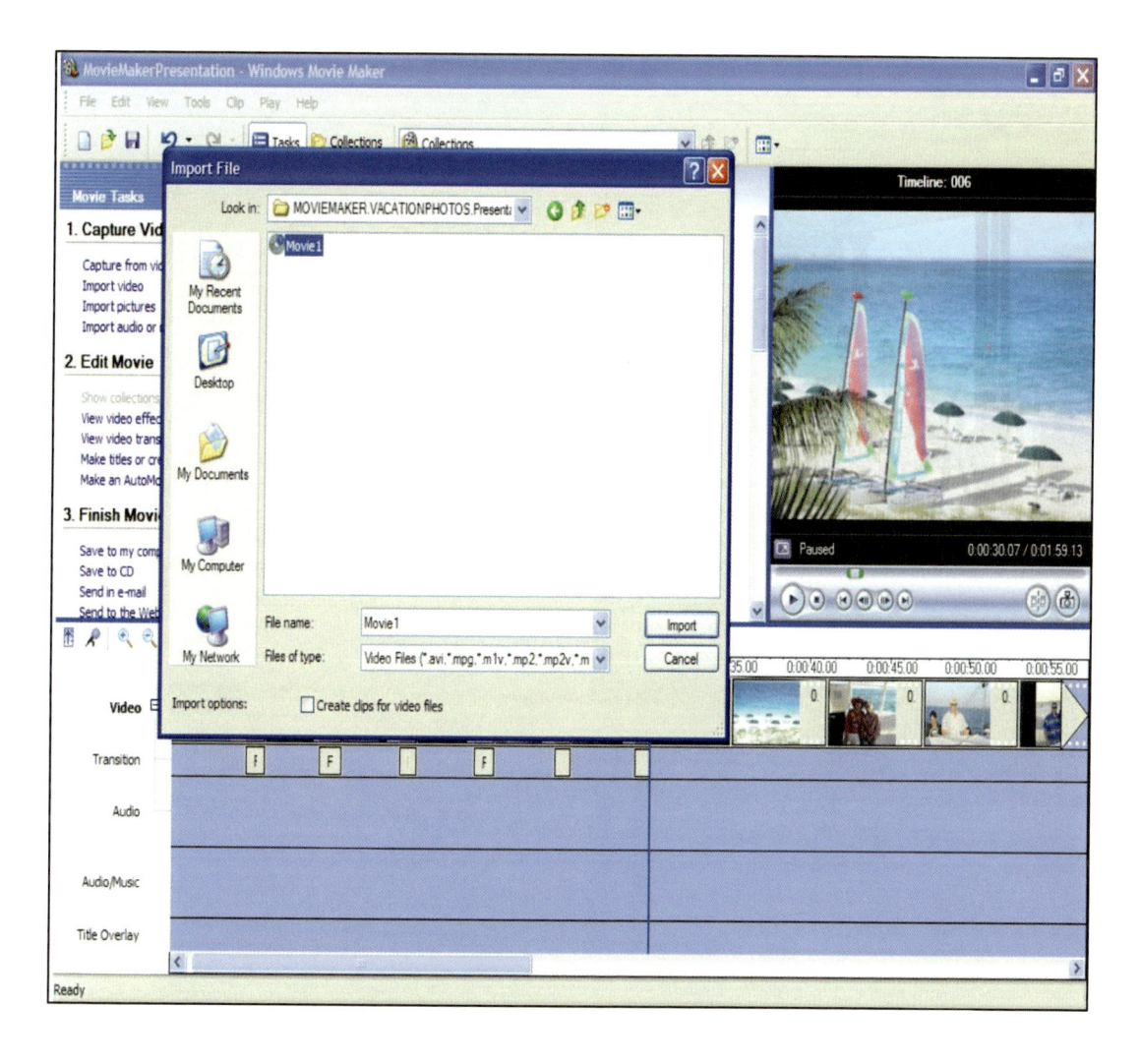

Movie Maker will import most video types.

Your video will appear in the COLLECTIONS area. Drag your video down to the place in which you want it in your slideshow.

By placing your cursor over the section of video, you can see the duration of the video—in this case 35.69 seconds.

> Don't forget to create a Fade/Overlap Transition between your Video clip and the images immediately before and after it.

If your video includes sound, the sound appears in the Audio section of the slideshow. If you're going to add music to this slideshow, you don't want the audio from the movie clip to interfere with that, so Mute the movie clip.

Do this by putting your cursor on the section of movie clip audio, *Right Click*, and from the dialogue box select MUTE.

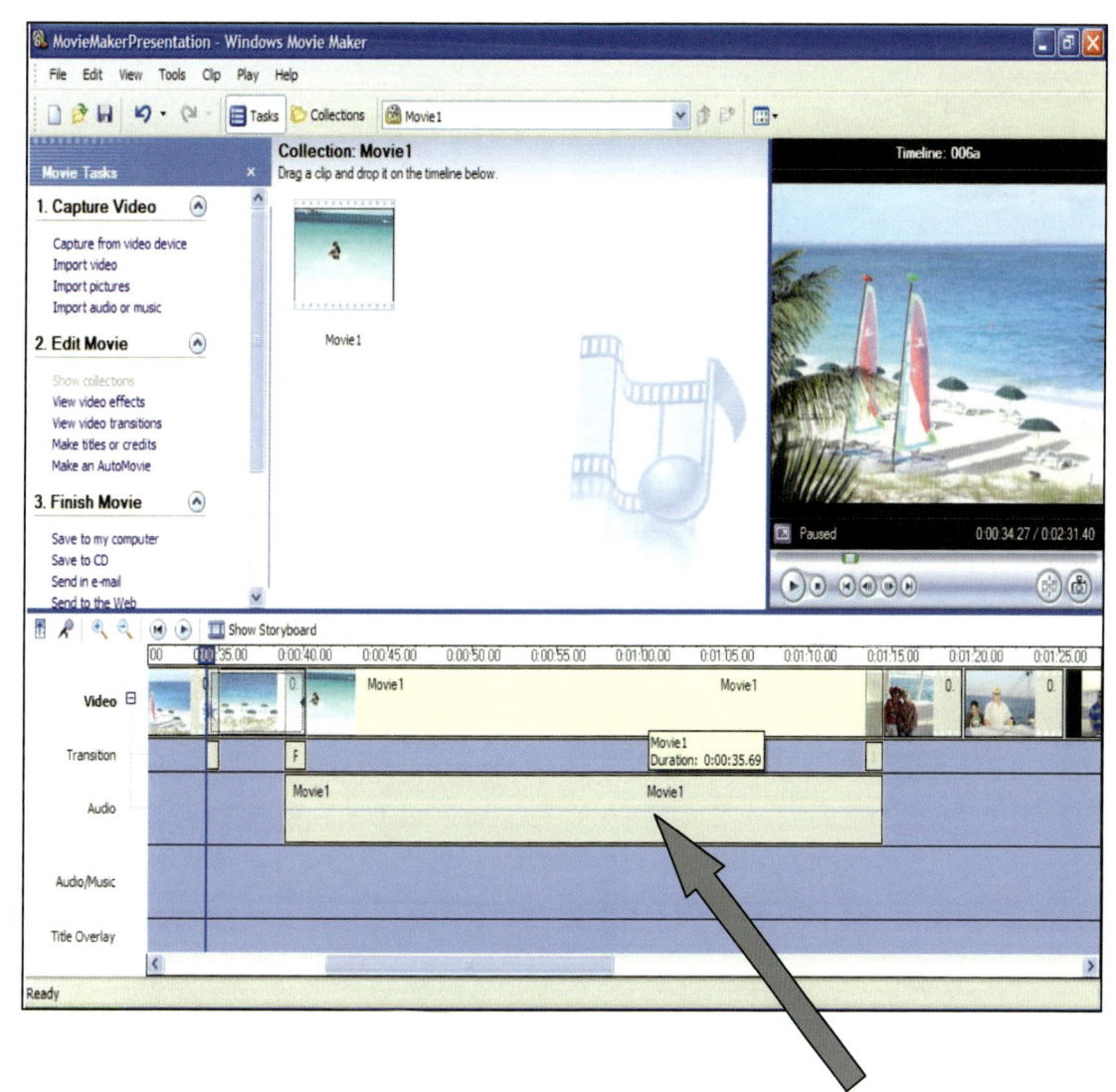

Mute the sound portion of your video clip.

MUSIC

Adding music to your DVD slideshow is also a lot of fun, and vital to creating a well-rounded, enjoyable presentation.

Go to IMPORT AUDIO OR MUSIC in your MOVIE TASKS section, click on it, and an import box will open. Find the file in which you store your music, make your selection, and import it to your slideshow.

> I think I should have no other mortal wants, if I could always have plenty of music. Life seems to go on without effort when I am filled with music."
> ~ George Eliot

35

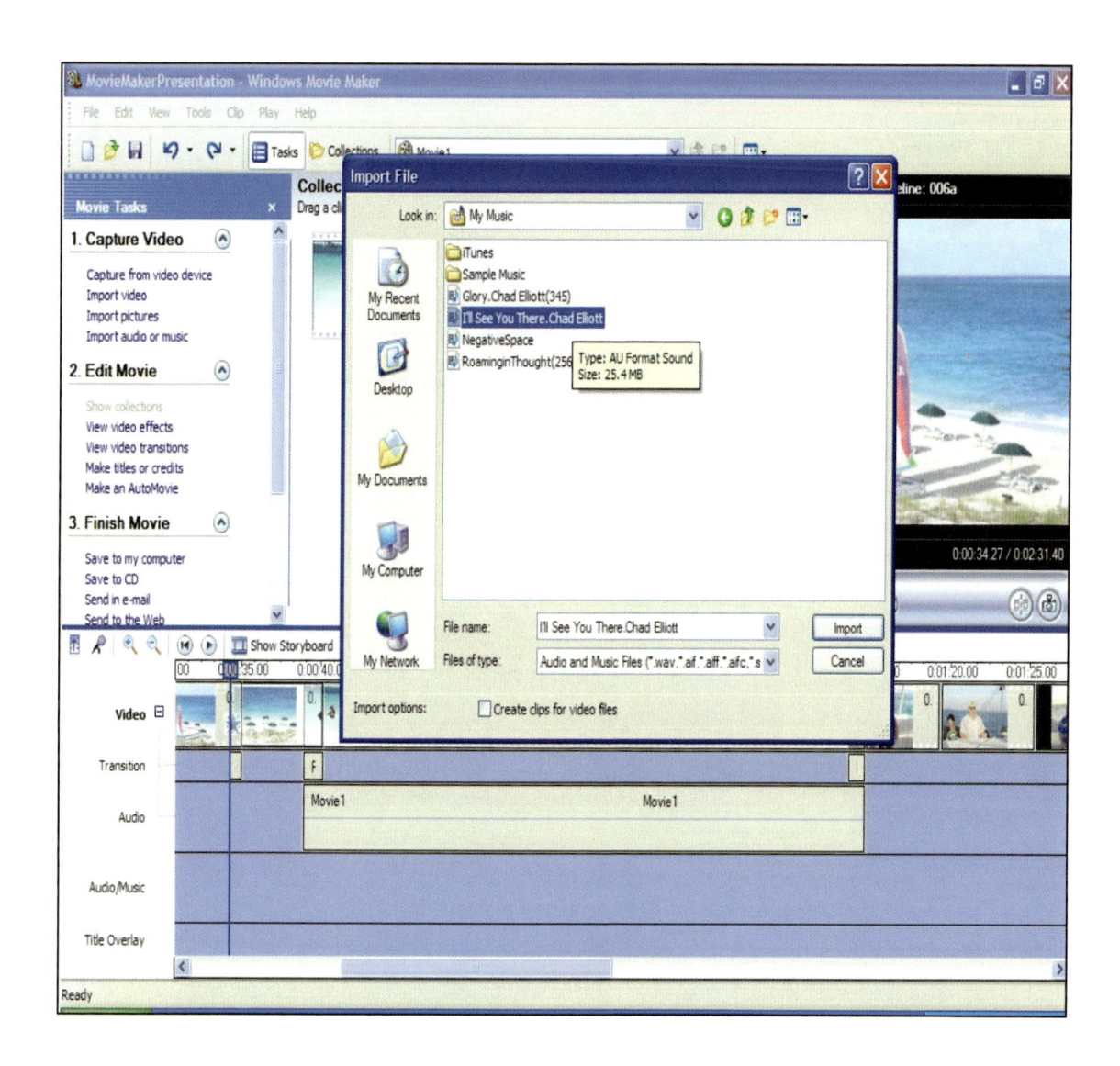

Once your music is imported, drag it down to the AUDIO/MUSIC section of your Storyboard.

Because music clips sometimes start rather abruptly, add a Fade-In, as with the Title Page. Put your cursor on the music, *Right Click*, and from the dialogue box choose Fade In.

If adding two or more songs to your slideshow, have them overlap slightly. You don't want a dead space of 2 – 3 seconds with no music in the middle of your movie. Add Fade In and Fade Out to the songs that overlap, so the transition is nice and smooth.

If you find you have too much music at the end of your slideshow, that it continues well after your images have ended, just put your cursor on the right edge of the final song and drag the end to the left until you reach the end of your images. Fade Out is especially important here to create a smooth ending to your slideshow.

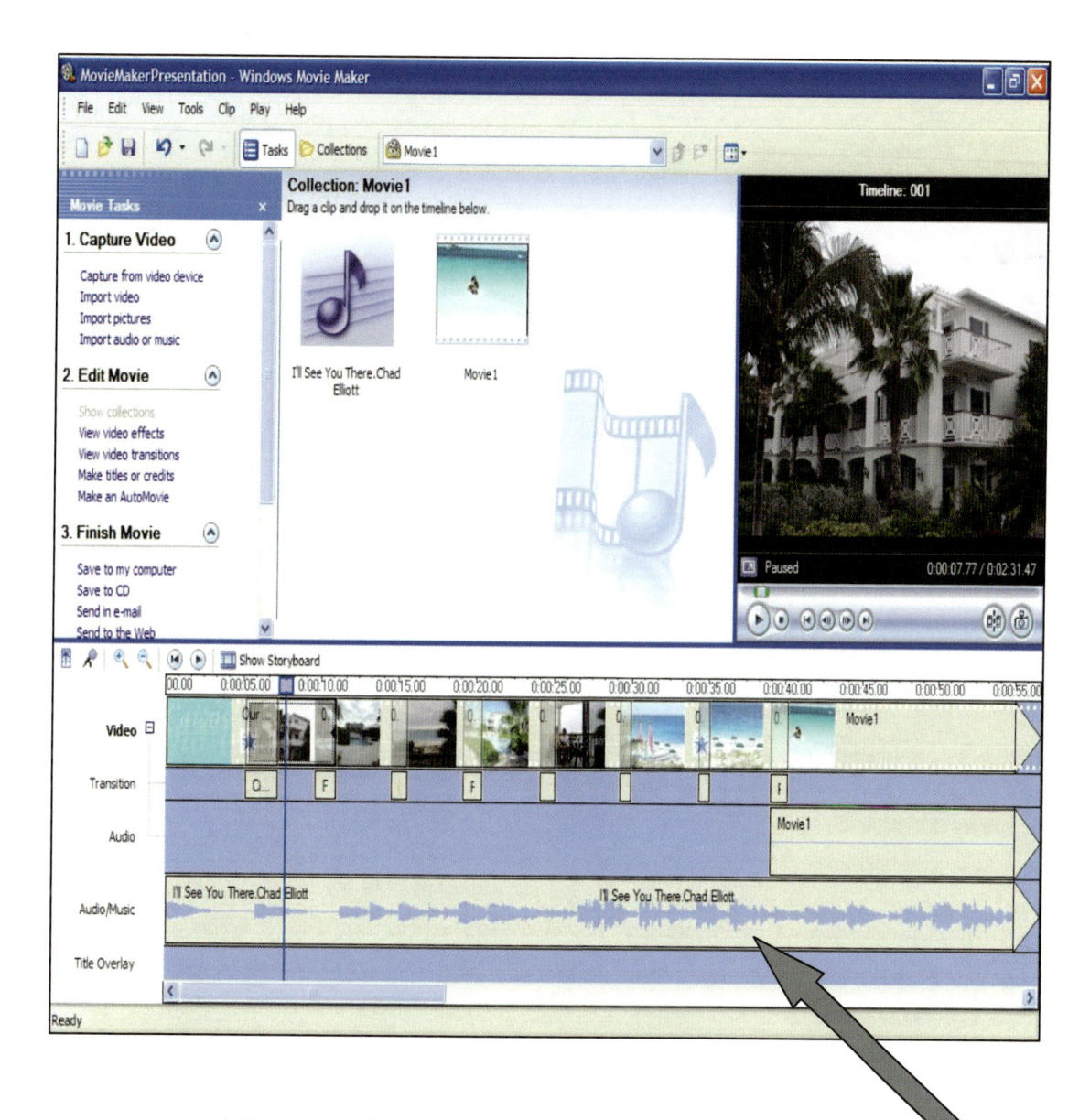

Adjust the volume of the music by right-clicking on it.
When the dialogue box opens, select Volume and make your adjustment.

NARRATION

Adding narration is a great way to personalize your slideshow and enhance your movie. You can record your own or others' words talking about your great trip or your special event.

Go to TOOLS, and in the drop-down choose NARRATE TIMELINE. Place your PLAYBACK INDICATOR on the spot in your slideshow where you want to start your narration.

> If you're using a PC you'll need a microphone, either a headset or the standing type. Computer microphones can be bought just about anywhere, and are fairly inexpensive.

Click START NARRATION when you're ready to begin. As you are recording you'll notice NARRATION CAPTURED is keeping track of the seconds as they tick by.

Click STOP NARRATION when you're finished. Movie Maker immediately brings up the SAVE WINDOWS MEDIA FILE, in which your Narration will most likely be called UNTITLED NARRATION. At this point name your Narration and choose the file in which you want to save it. Click SAVE.

Movie Maker will then automatically place your recorded narration in the slideshow timeline. But you're not locked into that spot. You can move the narration, if you wish, by placing your cursor on it and dragging it to a different place.

When you're satisfied with your Narration click on DONE, and you'll return to your working area, with the newly created Narration in place.

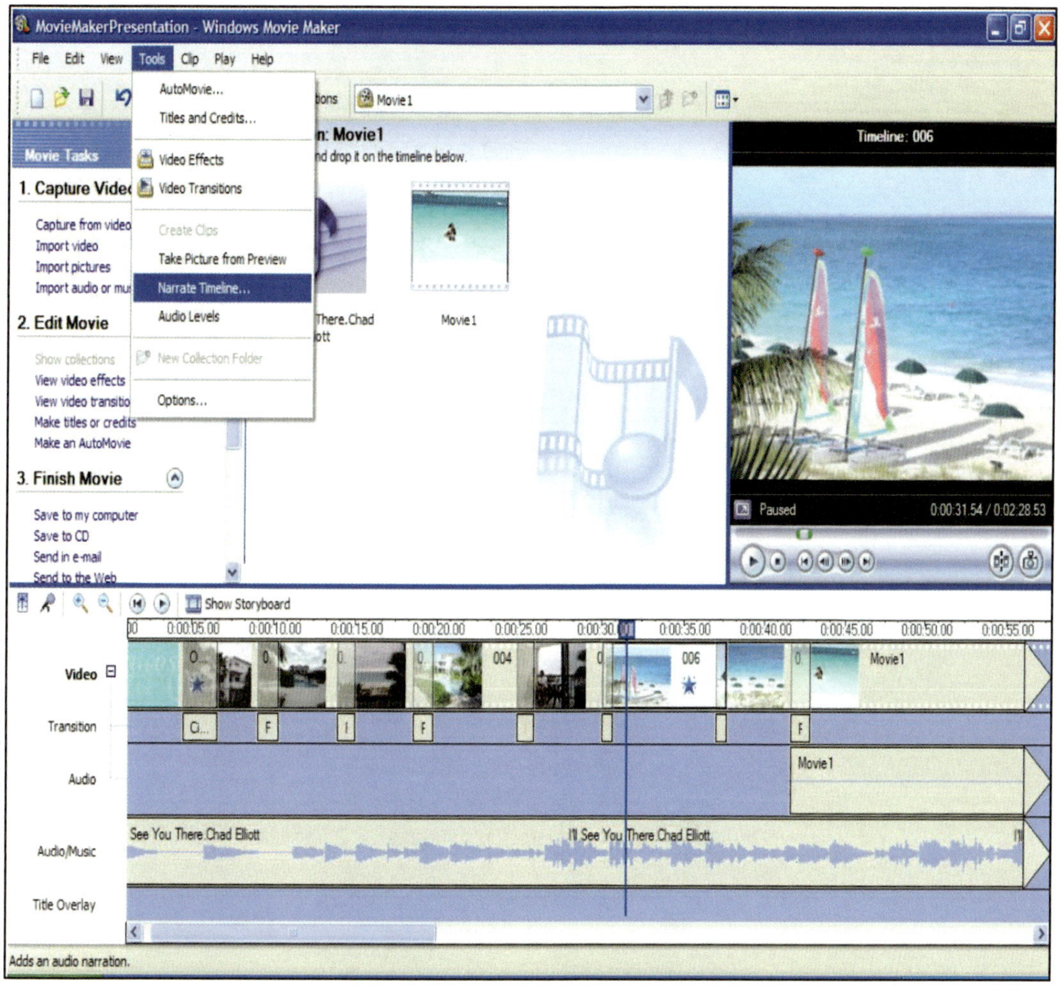
MovieMakerPresentation - Windows Movie Maker
File
Edit
View
Tools
Clip
Play
Help
AutoMovie...
Titles and Credits...
Video Effects
Video Transitions
Create Clips
Take Picture from Preview
Narrate Timeline...
Audio Levels
New Collection Folder
Options...
Movie1
Movie Tasks
1. Capture Video
Capture from video
Import video
Import pictures
2. Edit Movie
Show collections
View video effects
Make an AutoMovie
3. Finish Movie
Save to my computer
Save to CD
Send in e-mail
Send to the Web
Timeline: 006
Paused
0:00:31.54 / 0:02:28.53
Show Storyboard
Video
Transition
Audio
Audio/Music
Title Overlay
See You There Chad Elliott
I'll See You There Chad Elliott
Adds an audio narration.

END CREDITS

Your END CREDITS, like your Title, can be done a couple of different ways.

You can again click on MAKE TITLE OR CREDITS, and choose CREDITS AT THE END of the movie. This will create a final page similar to your Title at the beginning of your movie.

Or you can choose TITLE ON THE SELECTED CLIP. Again you will decide on Title Animation and Text Font and Color, just as you did with your Title page, only this time your ending message will appear superimposed on the final image in your slideshow.

> Drag the final image of your slideshow out so it appears for a longer duration than the previous images. Stretching out the time of that final image alerts your viewers that the end is near and creates a sense of completion.

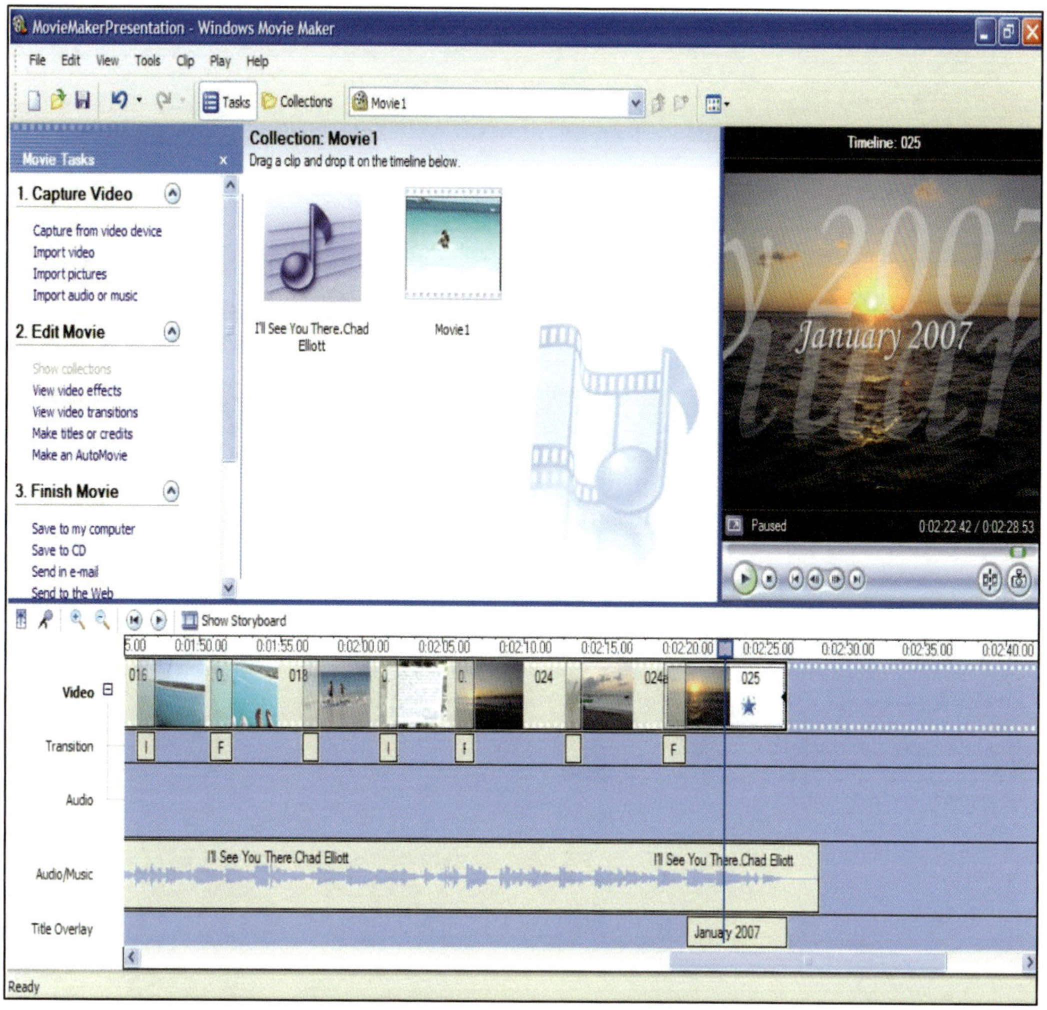
MovieMakerPresentation - Windows Movie Maker
File Edit View Tools Clip Play Help
Tasks
Collections
Movie 1
Movie Tasks
1. Capture Video
Capture from video device
Import video
Import pictures
Import audio or music
2. Edit Movie
Show collections
View video effects
View video transitions
Make titles or credits
Make an AutoMovie
3. Finish Movie
Save to my computer
Save to CD
Send in e-mail
Send to the Web
Collection: Movie1
Drag a clip and drop it on the timeline below.
I'll See You There.Chad Elliott
Movie1
Timeline: 025
January 2007
Paused
0:02:22.42 / 0:02:28.53
Show Storyboard
Video
Transition
Audio
Audio/Music
I'll See You There.Chad Elliott
Title Overlay
January 2007
Ready

SAVE YOUR MOVIE FILE

How long to make your slideshow/movie? Eight to ten minutes is a good length, and allows room for two to three songs. Depending on the duration of your individual images, a slideshow of eight minutes will hold approximately eighty to ninety images.

Longer than that, and you run the risk of your audience growing restless. Also, the longer your clip the more space it takes up on your computer. If you don't have plenty of RAM, this can cause your computer to show down or even freeze.

When you're satisfied with your slideshow, the next step will be to FINISH MOVIE. In your MOVIE TASKS you'll see SAVE TO MY COMPUTER. Click on this and a new box will open. This is where you name your movie, and also choose in which folder you wish to save it.

Click NEXT, and choose BEST QUALITY FOR PLAYBACK ON MY COMPUTER (RECOMMENDED).

With that box you'll also see MOVIE FILE SIZE, and below that ESTIMATED SPACE REQUIRED. This lets you know the approximate size your finished file will be after it's saved.

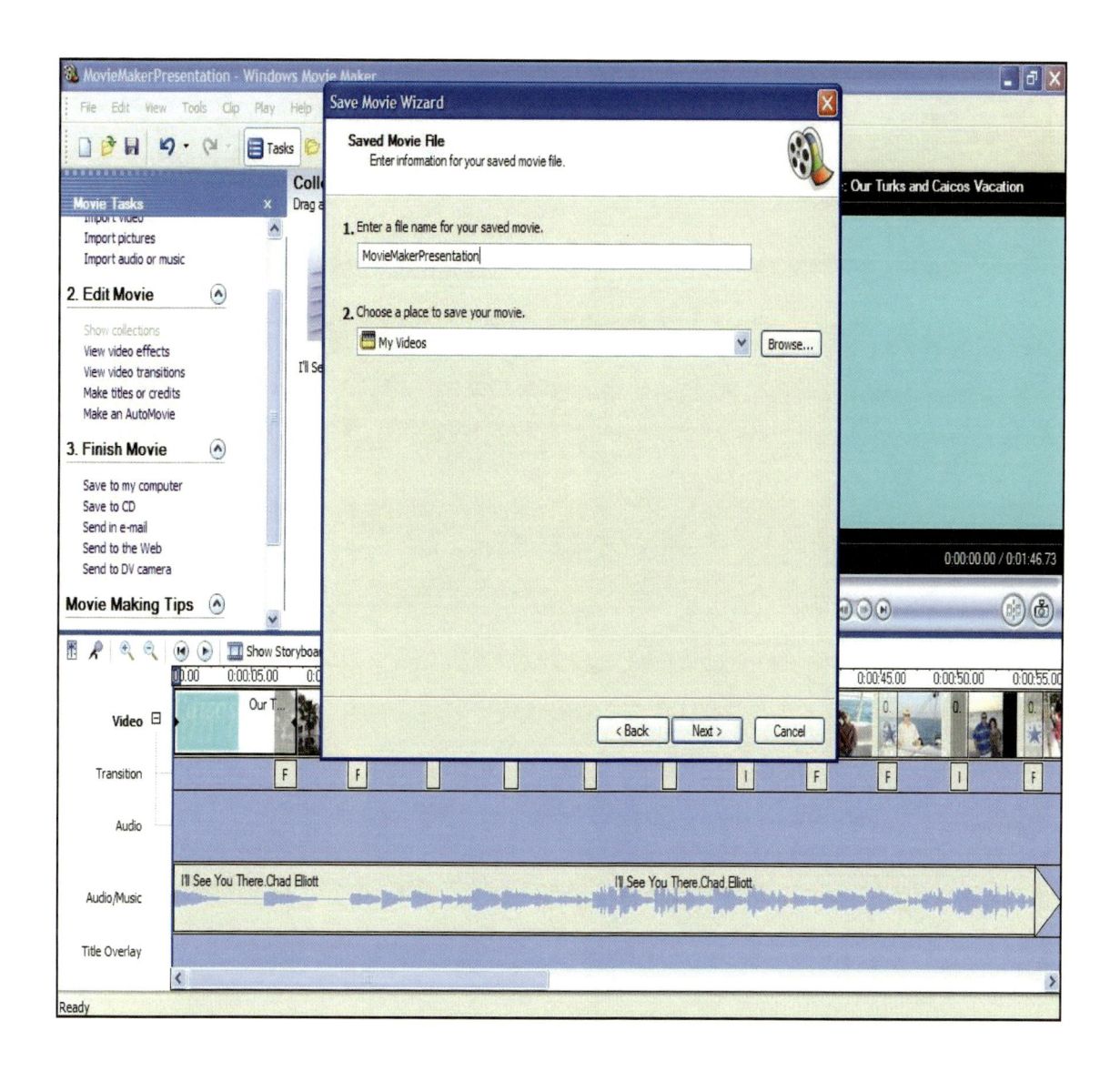

If you don't want to save your newly created movie in the default My Videos file, click on Browse, and select a different location.

Once you begin saving your movie, Movie Maker will keep you informed of the progress. Depending on your computer speed, the number of images and the duration of your slideshow, this can take from three to ten minutes, or even longer.

When the save is complete, you'll be informed that it's Finished, and you can now close the Movie Maker program.

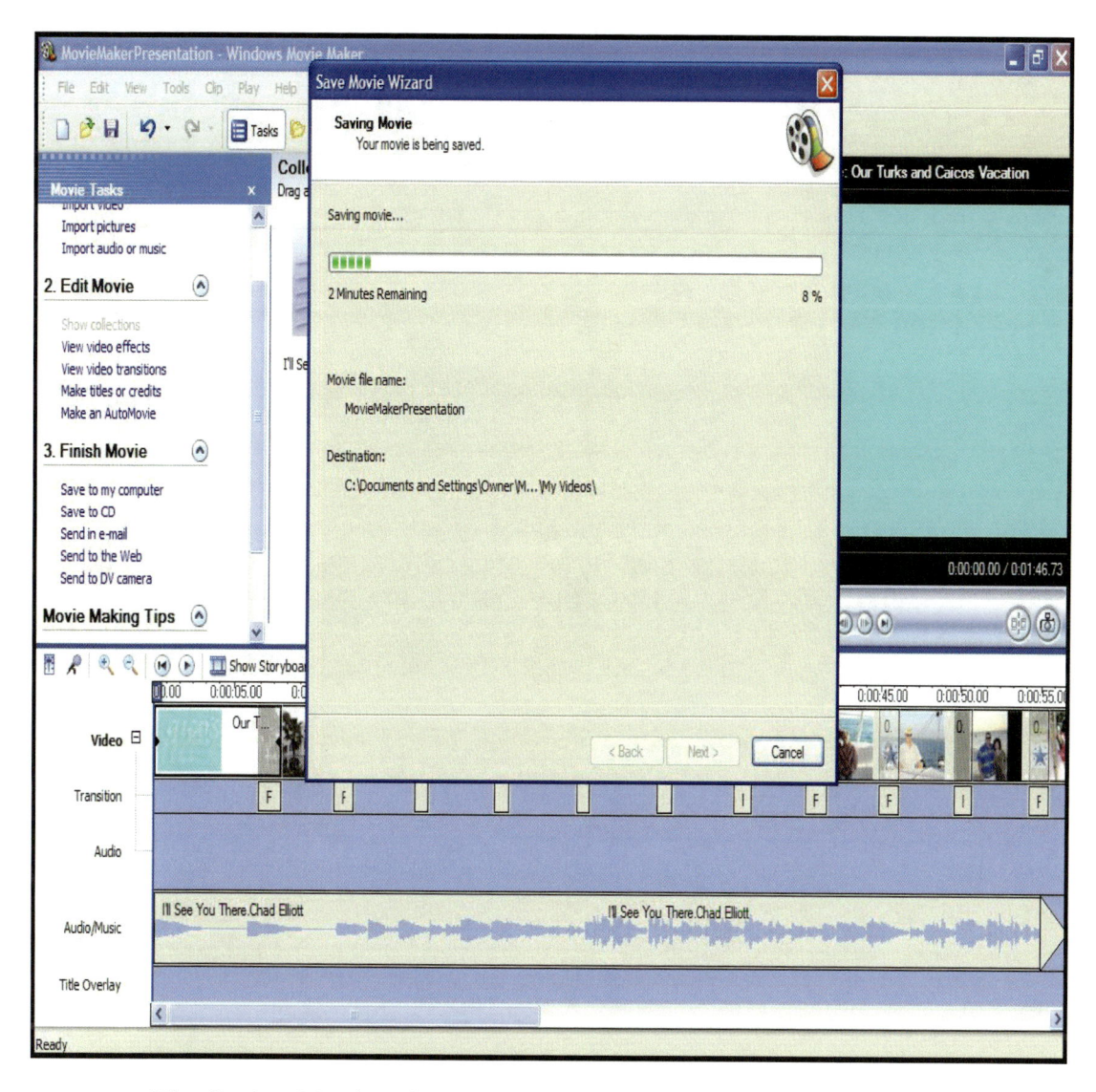

The Saving Movie Wizard will let you know how much longer it
will take to save your movie, as well as its destination.

BURN YOUR MOVIE TO A DVD

Congratulations, you've created a movie! If you want, you can keep the movie on your computer and watch it there, but half the fun of the Movie Maker program is that you can burn your newly created movie to a DVD for easier sharing—provided, of course, your computer has a DVD burner.

Most computers these days come with built-in DVD burning capabilities, but if yours doesn't have this feature it's easy to add. You can either take your PC to your local friendly computer store and have an internal DVD burner installed, buy an internal DVD burner and install it yourself (trickier), or buy an external DVD burner (most hover around the $100 price range) and plug it into your computer's USB port.

There are several different brands and types of DVDs onto which you can burn your DVD. I've tried most of them and have found little difference in quality. You can get DVD+R, DVD-R, or DVD+/-R. Through my own experimentation I've found DVD-R to be the most compatible with various different DVD players, but you'll want to try different types until you find the one that works best for you.

Now, find the DVD burning program on your computer. There are too many different brands for me to attempt to list them all here, but most are user-friendly and will walk you through the steps.

Be sure to look for Continuous Loop (usually in OPTIONS), and activate this feature. If you create a movie to play at an event—such as a graduation or anniversary party—you'll want the movie to play continuously until you stop it.

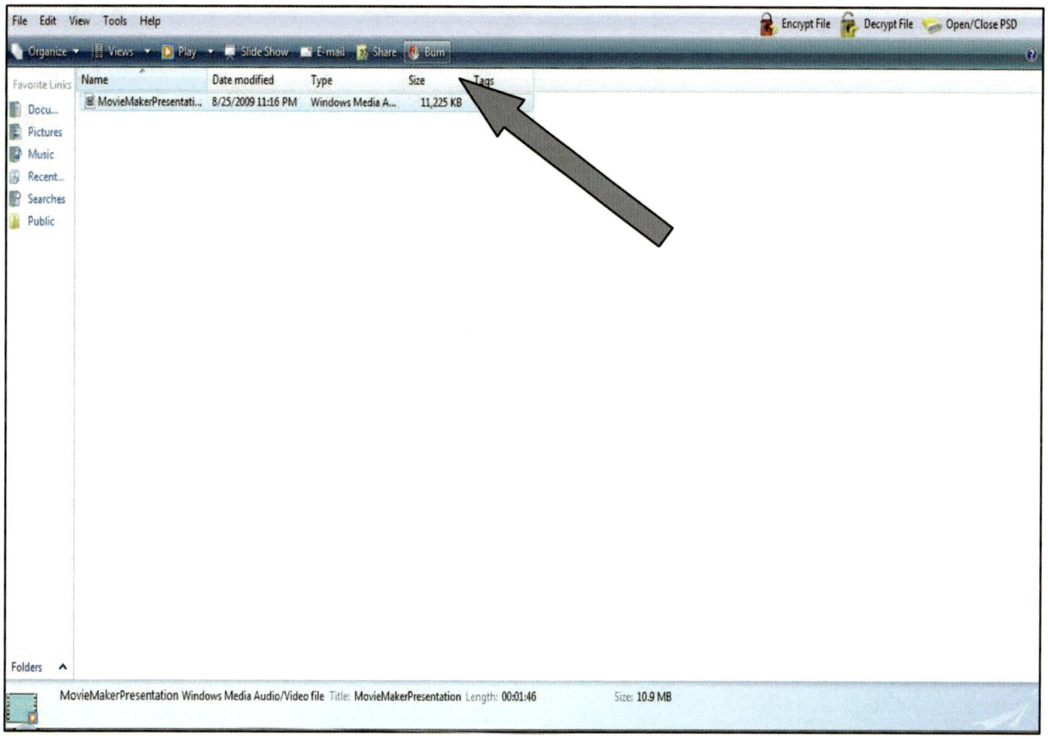
File Edit View Tools Help
Encrypt File
Decrypt File
Open/Close PSD
Organize
Views
Play
Slide Show
E-mail
Share
Burn
Favorite Links
Docu...
Pictures
Music
Recent...
Searches
Public
Name
Date modified
Type
Size
Tags
MovieMakerPresentati...
8/25/2009 11:16 PM
Windows Media A...
11,225 KB
Folders
MovieMakerPresentation Windows Media Audio/Video file Title: MovieMakerPresentation Length: 00:01:46
Size: 10.9 MB

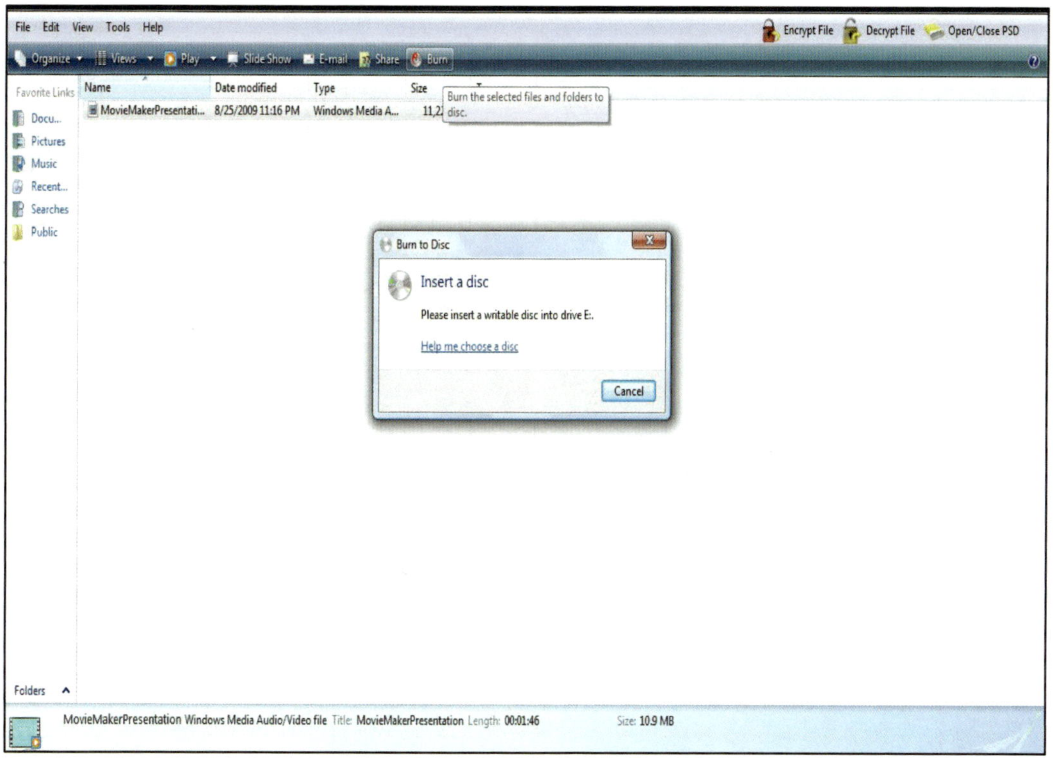
File Edit View Tools Help
Encrypt File
Decrypt File
Open/Close PSD
Organize
Views
Play
Slide Show
E-mail
Share
Burn
Favorite Links
Docu...
Pictures
Music
Recent...
Searches
Public
Name
Date modified
Type
Size
MovieMakerPresentati...
8/25/2009 11:16 PM
Windows Media A...
Burn the selected files and folders to disc.
Burn to Disc
Insert a disc
Please insert a writable disc into drive E:.
Help me choose a disc
Cancel
Folders
MovieMakerPresentation Windows Media Audio/Video file Title: MovieMakerPresentation Length: 00:01:46
Size: 10.9 MB

Ta-da! You now have a finished DVD of the movie you created, ready to share and impress your friends and family with your creativity and skill. Once you've created one movie you'll no doubt want to make many more. They make great gifts for all occasions.

There are a couple of more things you'll want to consider to go with your DVD. Any store with a video department will also have a selection of DVD/CD labels and label makers. Now that you have that wonderful movie, you'll want to put a nice label on it. Select one still image from the movie to use on the label, then simply give it a title and a date.

Also, you'll want a nice case in which to put your DVD. The square plastic cases are probably the most economical, but for a nice, professional look, I recommend buying the slim DVD cases that look like the ones in which professional DVDs come. These have a clear front and back pocket into which you can slide a cover made to match the DVD label you've created.

Have Fun!

Other books by Jean Tennant:

Knee High by the Fourth of July: More Stories of Growing Up in and Around Small Towns in the Midwest (editor)
Shapato Publishing, October 2009

Walking Beans Wasn't Something You Did With Your Dog: Stories of Growing Up in and Around Small Towns in the Midwest (editor)
Shapato Publishing, August 2008

Olivia's Birthday Puppy
Sweet Memories Publishing, May 2008

Under the name Jean Simon:

Ghost Boy
Kensington, 1994

Orphans
Kensington, 1992

Sweet Revenge
Kensington, 1991

Wild Card
Kensington, 1991

Darksong
Kensington, 1990

Descendants
Warner, 1989

Playing House
Silhouette, 1986

Made in the USA
Charleston, SC
08 May 2010